With this volume we begin what we hope will be the first publication in book form of the complete, uncut BARNABY, just as it first appeared in the pages of the old *PM* newspaper. Some eagle-eyed fans of BARNABY will notice that Barnaby and Mr. O'Malley begin in slightly different form from that of later episodes. As is true in all good strips, the characters here evolved as their creator, Crockett Johnson, grew to know them better and realize them more fully. Some of the strips were later redrawn, but we have chosen to be faithful to the original version throughout.

The Publisher wishes to thank her husband Lester del Rey for introducing her to Barnaby and Mr. O'Malley; Scott Meredith, the agent who always delivers, and his capable lieutenants, Jack Scovil and Jonathan Silverman; Bill Blackbeard, Director of the San Francisco Academy of Comic Art, who worked long and hard to provide us with copies of the original artwork; Don and Maggie Thompson for getting the word out; Ron Goulart for his enthusiastic support; Sidney Kramer of Mews Books, Ltd., who agreed to agree; and to all the fans who answered our query with wild and enthusiastic cries of, "Yes, bring back BARNABY! Do it! Do it!

BARNABY #1

Wanted: A Fairy Godfather

by
CROCKETT JOHNSON

A Del Rey Book
Ballantine Books • New York

A Del Rey Book
Published by Ballantine Books

Copyright © 1985 by Random House, Inc.

Library of Congress Catalog Card Number: 85-90761

ISBN 0-345-32673-3

Designed by Gene Siegel

Manufactured in the United States of America

First Ballantine Books Edition: November 1985

A TIME THERE WAS
(and not so long ago)

when the world was very different for a five-year-old boy with an active mind.

There was no *Sesame Street* to immobilize him before a screen where puppets and clowns made games of letters and numbers. There were no Saturday cartoons to stultify his imagination with cliché supermen and wild events unrelated to his experience. Indeed, there was no television to hold him from the activities his mind and body needed to develop his growing abilities fully.

There were stories his parents might tell him or read to him, but those required mental creativity to flesh out the words.

It was a safer time, when a child might be free to explore the local haunted house with delighted shudders or wander into nearby woods to climb trees, chase squirrels, or pretend the shadows hid Indians, dragons, or ogres.

The brief radio broadcasts were filled with something about a war, of course; but without pictures of battle horrors, these were of little interest to a child. Anyhow, most adults preferred to listen to Stella Dallas, Vic and Sade, Edgar Bergen and Charlie McCarthy, Fred Allen, or Mr. Anthony who always knew the answers.

For the adults, this was a time when the Office of Civil Defense (OCD) was busy protecting us from the danger of bombs falling out of the skies (carried somehow by planes that could never have made the long round trip). There were blackouts with drills, sirens, and a large corps of volunteer air raid wardens. In this simpler world, the atom and hydrogen bombs did not yet exist.

But there were shortages, caused by the need for many things that had to be sent to our armed forces and allies across the seas. Ration boards doled out coupons for gasoline, tires, sugar, meat, and many other scarce items. Scrap metal drives were instituted, and people were encouraged to start victory gardens.

Of course, the shortages quickly produced a black market, with goods often supplied by the hijacking of trucks by the criminal element. Even stolen ration coupons were available— for a price.

It was a busy time for both adults and young children. It was a time when many things were done—some of them silly and some that were highly important.

Unfortunately, in the frantic events of those days, the simple faith of a boy named Barnaby and the importance of his Fairy Godfather, Jackeen J. O'Malley, were largely ignored.

They should not have been...

* * *

(For a short history of *Barnaby* and Crockett Johnson, please turn to page 209.)

BARNABY #1

Wanted: A Fairy Godfather

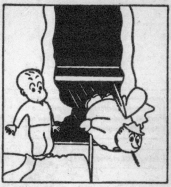

'Morning Mom . . . 'Morning Grandma . . . 'Morning Pop. Mr. O'Malley DID fly in my room last night. I found his cigar ashes!

4·24   Copyright, 1942, Marshall Field

He's my Fairy Godfather. He flew in my window and talked to me and he flew out into the flower bed . . .

Something DID get into the flower bed last night . . . Probably a dog.

Nobody believes in pixies any more, son.

Look at that flower bed! Clumsiest pixie I ever did hear of.

CROCKETT JOHNSON

You'll spot the enemy planes a long way off and fly down and tell me and I'll phone the army airport . . .? Very neat indeed, Mr. O'Malley!

5·2

CROCKETT JOHNSON

Pop, that was Mr. O'Malley, my Fairy Godfather. He's going to fly around nights so we can tell away ahead of time when an air raid is coming.

How nice! But hasn't the Army some plan for that?

Oh, Mr. O'Malley will spot them before the Army can. You air wardens can take things a little easier from now on, Pop.

Tell your Mr. O'Malley the ARP will be very grateful.

And now that we've had our little joke, son, suppose you tell me who that REALLY was on the phone.

It WAS Mr. O'Malley!

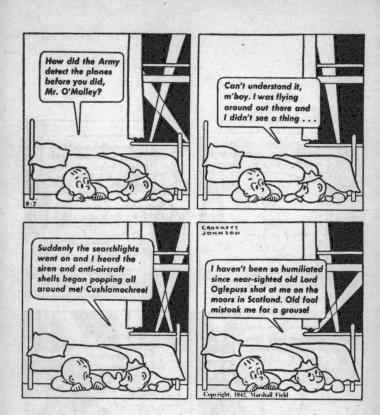

16

A dungeon!

Reminds me of the time I was incarcerated in a castle . . . .

Gosh!

5-14

Yes. Some varlet slammed the door of the wine cellar.

Well, you'd better hide here until we can prove you're not an enemy spy.

Yes, m'boy. I must remain here away from my beloved forests and vales. But don't worry about your poor old Fairy Godfather.

CROCKETT JOHNSON

O'Malley always makes the best of things . . .

JAM JAM JAM JAM JAM JAM

Nobody will know you're hiding here in the cellar, Mr. O'Malley. Just be quiet . . .

Quiet?

Quiet? Were you admonishing me, your Fairy Godfather, to be QUIET? Me, who can tear off forty winks in a cowslip's bell without disturbing a dewdrop!

Me, who can do a rhumba on a cobweb! Don't you ever read books? Be off with you, m'boy.

Gosh!

CROCKETT JOHNSON

Gosh, Mr. O'Malley, ruining Mom's preserves was practically sabotage. They were one of her war efforts.

M'boy, you wouldn't begrudge your old Godfather a bit of jam on his crust of bread, surely?

But you didn't have a crust of bread.

Ah, no. Your poor old Fairy Godfather didn't have even a dry crust of bread . . . Ah, well

We've got to prove you're not a dangerous enemy spy so you won't have to hide here in the cellar any longer. Maybe we could. . . .

Not even a tiny dry crust . . .

Oh, okay, okay . . .

Of course I was speaking only figuratively of that crust, m'boy. I trust it will be not too dry and not too tiny . . . and, er, perhaps garnished with a steak?

CROCKETT JOHNSON

Barnaby, I should like to bestow a boon upon this household in return for its hospitality.... Shall I rid the locality of werewolves? Charm the cattle and the crops against the ravages of evil spirits? ...

SOAP
5-20

We haven't any cattle and Pop's Victory garden is growing fine. And I don't think we've had much trouble with werewolves at all.

Then perhaps I can drive out snakes? Or witch a well? ..

Ah, that's it! I shall bestow the blessing of a never-failing water supply upon this plot of land ... Fetch me a forked stick, m'boy.

But we've got city water, Mr. O'Malley.

Not to be compared in taste with the clear, cool, beautiful nectar of the natural earth... Makes me thirsty merely to describe it ...

Er ... Is there any beer on ice, m'boy?

C.BCRNETT JOHNSON

Trust your old Fairy Godfather to find the best spot in the cellar for a well. Right handy to the stairs. Bring the pick.

Maybe Pop doesn't want a well.

Nonsense, m'boy. Your whole family will be delighted.

This well will put the city's water supply to shame. A few blows of the pick will usher up the coolest, clearest...

CROCKETT JOHNSON

I'll stroll in the backyard, m'boy, while you apprise your father of his staggering good fortune.

5-25

Pop! We've struck oil in the cellar!

That's fine, Barnaby.

Honest, Pop! It's a gusher! We're rich!

This IS oil on his hands.

What goes on here!

CROCKETT JOHNSON

31

Hello, Mr. O'Malley. I thought you stopped running away back there.

Puff!

5-29

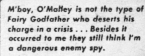

M'boy, O'Malley is not the type of Fairy Godfather who deserts his charge in a crisis . . . Besides it occurred to me they still think I'm a dangerous enemy spy.

Mr. O'Malley! If we could catch a real spy we'd be heroes. That would end all our troubles!

I daresay it would.

CROCKETT JOHNSON

I'll wish a real spy would happen to come right by here and you grant my wish and we'll catch him!

Er . . . Right HERE, m'boy?

Copyright, 1942, Marshall Field

35

41

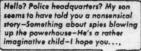

Hello? Police headquarters? My son seems to have told you a nonsensical story—Something about spies blowing up the powerhouse—He's a rather imaginative child—I hope you....

6-6

Copyright 1942, Marshall Field

Oh—Squad cars have left already —Oh—Yes, of course you have to act on any sort of tip nowadays —I can't say how sorry—But...

Well, Barnaby has got us in a mess this time. We'll probably spend the night explaining to the police.

There's a police car in the drive, dear!

Well, here it comes!

CROCKETT JOHNSON

It's the Chief of Police! This is even more serious than I imagined!

Ahem! I understand it was your boy who phoned us about spies who planned to blow up the powerhouse?

Er, yes— you see, he...

Did you catch them, Chief? Before the bombs went off?

Barnaby! Go back to bed!

CROCKETT JOHNSON Copyright 1942, Newfield Field

Yes, lad! We caught them all! And before the bombs went off!

Hey, Mom! What's the matter with Pop?

Thanks to this level-headed boy of yours, the spies are behind bars and the power for our city's war industries is saved! Great work!

Yes, sir! You keep your wits about you, don't you? No day dreaming or wool gathering for you, eh lad?

I shouldn't get all the credit, Chief. My..

You must excuse Barnaby. He should have been asleep hours ago. We'll hear his story in the morning.

Hey!

I was going to tell the Chief about Mr. O'Malley, my Fairy Godfather!

For once, we're going to leave your Mr. O'Malley out of the conversation, wings and all!

CROCKETT JOHNSON

I should have liked to hear your young hero tell how he discovered the bomb plot.

I think I can give you the gist of his story, Chief.

Barnaby, nobody will believe that you and your Fairy Godfather met a parrot who said the powerhouse was going to be blown up tonight. You just can't tell stories like that.

I suppose it does sound a little out of the ordinary.

CROCKETT JOHNSON

Copyright. 1942. Marshall Field

—So my son—not showing a semblance of fear—crept closer to the conspirators—all of them desperate men, armed to the teeth! Then—

We'll turn him over to the FBI in the morning Mr. O'Malley, and he'll repeat everything he heard the spies planning.

Polly wants a cracker!

Not a bad idea he has there, Barnaby. A little midnight snack from the pantry would...

Mr. O'Malley!

Polly wants a cracker!

HE'S LOST HIS NAZI ACCENT!

CROCKETT JOHNSON

Good morning, son. The paper is full of you and the spies you helped catch ... There's your picture...

Doesn't flatter me any, does it, Mom?

Of course the case isn't closed yet. When Mr. O'Malley makes that Nazi parrot talk we'll nab a lot more spies ... Let's you and I go see how he's made out, Pop.

Huh?

You mean you've got your Fairy Godfather cross-examining a parrot for the FBI in our cellar? Why don't you rest on your laurels?

Go ahead, Pop. Mr. O'Malley is quite interested in meeting you.

Mr. O'Malley and the parrot! They're not here! Gosh, Pop! I'm worried!

Not as worried as I'd be, son, if they WERE!

51

Barnaby has been so unhappy since he imagined his Fairy Godfather disappeared that I almost wish he would imagine him back again.

My gosh, not THAT!

No, son. I haven't any idea what has happened to your Mr. O'Malley . . . Maybe he's been drafted.

They won't take him. He's only my size.

Not tall enough, eh? He found that out when he tried to enlist, I suppose.

CROCKETT JOHNSON

No, I did.

55

I'll have to talk to Mr. O'Malley about him going away like this.

It's bedtime, Barnaby.

You'd think a Fairy Godfather would let me know— phone me or something— send a postcard.

Something drastic has got to be done! I'll end this pixie nonsense!

Where are you going?

I'm going to mail Barnaby a postcard— from Mr. O'Malley!

This card has the national capitol on it. It says: "Called out of town on secret business. Will be away a year or two... Your Fairy Godfather."

I know. I sen—I mean—read the OTHER card!

It's a picture of some awful bar and grill called Paddy's. "Hello, my boy. Back soon. Keep 'em flying. O'Malley."

Looks like a very high class place to me, Mom.

Who in the world would send a child a fake postcard like that!

Pretty low trick, isn't it, Pop? If that genuine card hadn't arrived too...

...I might actually have gone around for a couple of years believing I didn't have a Fairy Godfather!

CROCKETT JOHNSON

It's not because Barnaby dreams he has a Fairy Godfather. I'm worried because he won't admit it's only a dream...

Well, we can't sit up all night worrying.

He believes this O'Malley creature is as real as you or I am—Say! Here's an idea!

If we could wake him right in the middle of one of his dreams we'd surely convince him...

Sshh! Barnaby is talking in his sleep!

GOSH, I'M SURE GLAD YOU'RE BACK, MR. O'MALLEY...

Here's our chance!

60

Barnaby is dreaming again about that Fairy Godfather of his. Sshh!

Gee, that's wonderful, Mr. O'Malley.

Barnaby. I've brought you a pony!

Gosh! Pop can put the car up now!

I thought you might like these Seven League Boots. They're genuine rubber.

But, Mr. O'Malley, Leon Henderson...

Copyright 1942, World 2 Pub.

And right here, m'boy, is the biggest caramel sundae in the world!

Hey! I bet this is all a DREAM!

CROCKETT JOHNSON

Maybe you're not lost, Mr. O'Malley, but I am.

Lost? With your Fairy Godfather leading you? Preposterous, Barnaby!

We'll rest here a bit, then I shall guide you, like an arrow, out of this forest.

But maybe we should have been dropping breadcrumbs or . . .

M'boy, I resent . . . Say! What does that absurd bird think he's doing?

Mr. O'Malley! He's a robin!

Copyright, 1942, PM Syndicate

HE'S TRYING TO COVER US WITH LEAVES!

CROCKETT JOHNSON

That bird! Covering us with leaves!

That's what happened to those people in the book when they got lost in the woods.

And in another book an Ogre got them.

Well, take your Fairy Godfather's word for it, there aren't any supernatural creatures like Ogres running around. Not in this day and age ...

Gosh, Mr. O'Malley. You sound like Pop.

Ogres! What nonsense ... And besides, we're NOT LOST! But I'll ask the first Woodnymph we meet how to get out of this forest. She may know a shortcut.

Copyright, 1943, Ass Bundhand

CROCKETT JOHNSON

73

Wonderful dinner the Ogre put up, wasn't it, m'boy? ... Considering he only had an egg in his whole larder.

Let's offer to help with the dishes and get out of here, Mr. O'Malley.

We don't wash dishes, child. Hee, hee.

They're gone! Gosh, if Mom had an egg like that ...

Say, B.O., here's a trick that will amaze you ... Take a card ... Take any card ...

Perhaps later, O'Malley. I'd like to talk to you now—hee, hee—alone!

CROCKETT
JOHNSON

You'll pardon us, won't you, m'boy... Your Godfather has a bit of business to transact in B.O.'s conference room.

Oh, my gosh! Be careful, Mr. O'Malley!

Barnaby! You frightened me! How did you get in so quietly? Where have you been? What are you doing with that egg?

Huh?

7-22

I'll put it back in the icebox.

Grandma! That's a magic egg! It does things! It takes you places!

CROCKETT JOHNSON

Grandma put my magic egg in the icebox! I got it from the Ogre! He captured me and Mr. O'Malley, my Fairy Godfather! I just escaped . . .

RING

Don't answer the door, Pop! It's the Ogre after his egg!

In a Western Union uniform?

He's disguised!

"Copyright 1943, PM Syndicate"

81

It's a telegram from the home office. They want us to put up Mr. Jones, our chief production engineer, while he's in town.

It seems he's a nervous type and he can't stand hotels. I'm afraid we'll have to wire him an invitation. He's a pretty important nabob and I...

Gosh! If he's nervous ... and that Ogre comes for his egg—

Listen, Barnaby. While Mr. Jones is here, there'll be no talk about Ogres and magic eggs and Fairy Godfathers ... Promise me that.

Okay, Pop, but we'll just be living in a fool's paradise ...

CROCKETT JOHNSON

82

Who is the Ogre doing this important War work for? Our side or the Axis?

Cushlamochree!

No! It can't be!

7-27

You're acquiring a suspicious nature, m'boy. Would you like to accompany your Fairy Godfather to Bilharzia's house and have him reassure you?

He can't hurt us if we take the magic egg along. . . It's in the icebox, Mr. O'Malley.

I'll see if everybody's asleep. Mom is a little finicky about me going out in the middle of the night. . .

Everything's okay.

Barnaby.

CROCKETT JOHNSON

Copyright, 1942, PM Syndicate

Which of these two dozen colcareous ova would you say is the Druid's egg?

Laaban, laaban Take us near the Ogre's house . . . Not TOO near!

Gosh, we're there—I mean, HERE!

Cushlamochree! This is the way to travel, isn't it, m'boy? No air pockets or ceilings . . .

I'll put the bowl in the fork of this tree. The Druid's egg will be safe there while I prove to you that your fear of the Ogre is unfounded.

Mr. O'Malley! The Ogre is talking on the radio!

CROCKETT JOHNSON

Tell the mob in the Schwarzwald I'll start messing things up over here as soon as I get my Druid's egg back. I sent the brat's Fairy Godfather after it. I hired him.

He's radioing Germany!

He's a little windbag with wings named O'Malley. I'll make him sprinkle glass on roads, turn on lights during blackouts—things like that. If he gets too nosey . . .

. . . I'll eliminate him! And that ugly brat, too! Hee, hee, hee, hee, hee.

Cushlamochree!

Well, m'boy, our suspicion was justified! I'll tell that Ogre what I think of him as I tender my resignation.

. . . By mail!

That Ogre! Working for Hitler! And attempting to involve your Fairy Godfather in his nefarious schemes!

He can't do anything without the magic egg. Fly up there and say the magic words and get us away from here.

We have the Druid's egg even if we don't know which of these two dozen it is.

We'll plan a campaign— Hurry up, Mr. O'Malley, I heard a door open!

. . . Laaban, laaban—Say! Something's wrong, m'boy.

We're still here! It's not working!

Aha! Hee, hee!

CROCKETT JOHNSON

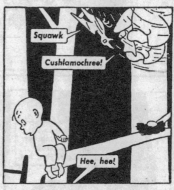

93

Don't get up, Barnaby. I flew by to see if you escaped safely from the Ogre ... Part of my Fairy Godfather service.

Hello, Mr. O'Malley. That bird who was chasing you, did ...

8-6

I outwitted her . . . I take it you brought back the magic Druid's egg?

Gosh, no . . . I guess it's still in that bird's nest. I just said the magic words. I didn't hold it.

But the Ogre thinks you have it. As I flew over his shack he shouted something about getting his egg back if he had to level your house to the ground in his search for it.

Gosh!

I bet Pop's insurance policy doesn't take in damage by Ogres!

CROCKETT JOHNSON

Copyright, 1942, PM Syndicate

Gosh, Mr. O'Malley, we can't have that Ogre coming around here in a temper and levelling the house to the ground . . . I promised Pop nothing'd happen while Mr. Jones was visiting us!

Never promise more than you can deliver, m'boy.

We've got to do something! .Mr. Jones arrives tomorrow. He's a nabob or something in Pop's company. He's nervous. Hotels always upset him . . .

Nervous? I'll cure him of that in an hour, Barnaby. I know things that MD's haven't dreamed of . . .

Anyway I promised Pop . . .

Nervousness. Let's see now . . . Name of the remedy has slipped my mind. . . Fellow on the radio spoke highly of it—VERY highly.

Well, I must be off now. Leave Mr. Jones and the Ogre to me, m'boy. Your Fairy Godfather will fix everything . . . I promise!

Copyright, 1962, PM Syndicate

CROCKETT JOHNSON

Barnaby, Mr. Jones has arrived to stay with us. He's in the living room now with your father.

Mr. Jones, the nervous nabob from Pop's central office?

Now, remember. No talk about Fairy Godfathers and Ogres. Go in and say how do you do and come right out.

Okay, Mom . . . But do you know what that awful Ogre said he'd do? He . . . Oh, okay.

It's a great pleasure to meet you and have you stay with us, Mr. Jones . . . I'd like to present my son, Barnaby.

Well, well. How do you do, little man. Hee, hee, heh.

CROCKETT JOHNSON

RUN, MOM! . . . IT'S THE OGRE!

Copyright, 1943, PM Syndicate

Barnaby! You're embarrassing us terribly! Mr. Jones is an important executive in your father's company! He's not someone in your dreams!

He's the Ogre!

Mom! Honest! He's not Mr. Jones!

You've never SEEN Mr. Jones before!

But I've seen the Ogre!

My, my! What has upset the little man?

Yeow!

He's—er—a little shy yet, Mr. Jones . . . When he gets to know you . . .

Oh, I'm sure Barnaby and I will get on just splendidly . . . Hee, hee . . . HEH

CROCKETT JOHNSON Copyright 1942 Field Publications

If we had the magic egg we could make the Ogre vanish! We've got to get it out of that bird's nest!

Precisely my idea!

Get away without the Ogre seeing you, m'boy. We'll meet at the tree.

Okay, Mr. O'Malley.

Nobody saw me leave . . . can't let that Ogre suspect my Fairy Godfather and I know he's not Mr. Jones . . .

Going for a walk, my little man? Hee, hee, heh. You won't mind if old Mr. Jones comes along, too . . .

CROCKETT JOHNSON

Copyright 1942 Field Publications

What's the matter, Barnaby? You look like you'd seen a banshee.

The Ogre! He was here! He's gone!

B-17   Copyright 1943 Field Publications

He must have followed me here! When I came down the ladder he was standing right here! He took the Druid's egg away from me ...

Cushlamochree!

Then when you were telling how you were going to say the magic words, you SAID them ... and you waved your hand over the magic egg! The Ogre had it in his hand!

You mean it WORKED? We're rid of the Ogre?

CROCKETT JOHNSON

Just shows the speed with which your Fairy Godfather accomplishes things, doesn't it, m'boy ... Can't keep up with my own achievements!

Mom. You'll probably be interested to know Mr. Jones won't be having any dinner with us . . . It turned out I was right about him being the Ogre . . . So we made him disappear . . . by magic!

I figured as long as you've got an extra place set, you might ask Mr. O'Malley to dinner . . . He's waiting out on the porch.

Barnaby, tell your dad and Mr. Jones dinner is just about ready . . .

Nobody will take my word for anything around this place . . . Maybe Mr. O'Malley, my Fairy Godfather, can get Mom to understand that there isn't any Mr. Jones any more!

Hello, my little man. Hee, hee, heh.

Mr. Jones!

CROCKETT JOHNSON

Gosh, Mr. O'Malley. I actually SAW the Ogre disappear. How did he get back in the house disguised as Mr. Jones from Pop's company?

An invisible Ogre could hardly use an invisible magic egg. Or could he?

If a visible egg could make him invisible, an invisible egg could make him VISIBLE.

Very weak metaphysics, Barnaby. There might be any number of sound, scientific explanations.

Possibly HYPNOTISM . . . I once saw a letter in the London Times . . . retired colonel . . . spent years in India, and while he never saw anything very unusual there himself, it seems he had this friend, whose cousin saw a—

Listen! Mr. Jones and Pop!

Yes, Mr. Jones, I'll have all my plans for the new factory sent here for you to look over . . .

Gosh! Pop's plans! . . . He must have hypnotized Pop!

CROCKETT JOHNSON

Come down here, Barnaby! You didn't put the frog in Mr. Jones' bed last night, did you. Oh, no! Nor the brambles in his pillow, nor the mousetrap in his shoe . . .

. . . nor the ink in his hair tonic! I suppose Mr. O'Malley, your fine Fairy Godfather, did all that!

Gosh! How did you ever find out, Mom?

I'm not through with you, young man! The way you've treated an important man in your father's firm! Mr. Jones came here for peace and quiet! I'm sure he'll leave the minute he checks those factory plans. He won't be able to get away from here fast enough!

Hee, hee, heh!

CROCKETT JOHNSON

TIMETABLE

Mom, you know how stubborn Pop is. I think you once passed a remark about it. Well, I can't convince him Mr. Jones is a Nazi Ogre. He's going to send Mr. Jones those plans from his office . . .

Mr. O'Malley, my Fairy Godfather, thinks very highly of you, Mom. He says when the messenger brings those plans you'll never give them to Mr. Jones on account of your intuition . . . He knew of a case . . .

There's the doorbell.

RING

Here's the package you've been waiting for, Mr. Jones.

Oh, thank you. I'll take it to my room.

MR. O'MALLEY!

MIS-TER O-MAL-LEY!

CROCKETT JOHNSON

Barnaby, I have a few pieces of soiled linen in this bag . . . I thought, perhaps, when your family laundry is being . . .

Mr. O'Malley! The Ogre has the plans! He must be getting ready to skip!

I wonder how he'll get past Mom with his suitcase . . . She'll be suspicious . . .

Well, a friend of mine—really he's only an acquaintance—occasionally finds himself in a very similar predicament . . .

He saunters out of his rooming house as though he was going for a pleasant stroll. But first he packs his suitcase and throws it from his window. Then—

Gosh!

Gosh!

CROCKETT JOHNSON

112

So this Nazi throws the bag out the window and nobody knows he's skipping ... But the kid here lugs it in the back door ... Then while the rat is looking for the bag, we come up, and he's got to scram without the plans ... Sure is a smart kid you got ...

But ...

8:28

Yes, officer. He's an exceptional child ... All the blueprints are in this bag! Not only mine but everything Jones took from the main office files ...

I've got to phone the president of the firm!

Hey, lady ...

CROCKETT JOHNSON Copyright 1942 Field Publications

What's the kid spouting about some Ogre conking his Godfather with a bag of laundry and trying to snatch some magic egg named O'Malley?

The excitement has upset him, officer.

But ...

All the blueprints are here! ... Yes, every one of them! ... Well, I'll tell you ... I rather suspected that man Jones from the beginning ... Not of being an Axis agent exactly, but ...

Shhh, Barnaby. Your father's telling the president of his company about the way you saved all the plans.

But Mr. O'Malley, my Fairy Godfather, is lying out there wounded ... Probably getting pneumonia and gangrene ...

Son, why must you always imagine ...

Let's humor him, dear. He's hysterical ... I'll get my first aid kit ...

Well, Barnaby. Where is our patient ... ?

Something's happened to him! He's gone!

CROCKETT JOHNSON

120

... This doctor is a child psychologist and he specializes in the problem of the imaginative child ... He may be able to help Barnaby get rid of his obsession that this Fairy Godfather he dreams about is a real person ...

Let's not rush into anything like that ... It must be normal for a child to have an imagination ... Barnaby's is just a bit more vivid than the average child's and—

Hey, Pop!

CROCKETT JOHNSON

I just phoned the Fire Department. Mr. O'Malley, my Fairy Godfather is stuck in a tree down the road and we need the hook and ladder ... Oh, by the way, Pop, Mr. O'Malley has lost his memory. Do you know a—

Huh?

What's the name of that doctor? I'm making an appointment NOW!

Gosh. Thanks, Pop. Mr. O'Malley will be very grateful.

Gosh!

Barnaby, in the bottom right hand corner of your mother's icebox is a cold leg of lamb—

MR. O'MALLEY! YOU'VE GOT YOUR MEMORY BACK!

Gosh! I better run home and phone the Fire Department . . . They don't have to get you down from the tree now . . . Are you sure you're all right?

. . . And while you're about it, m'boy, put a bit of your grandmother's fine homemade chow chow on those lamb sandwiches . . . It's on the third shelf in the pantry, near the cookies .

Gosh! He's all right, all right!

Copyright 1942 Field Publications

CECH MET JOHNSON

Calling out the Fire Department to save his imaginary Fairy Godfather who can't get down from a tree because he has amnesia and has forgotten how to fly! I hope this child psychologist we're taking Barnaby to knows his business!

I feel guilty about letting Barnaby believe we're seeing the doctor about the mythical O'Malley's loss of memory, but it's better that way. Barnaby will talk freely . . .

Pop!

Cancel the appointment! Mr. O'Malley cured himself! He got his memory back!

But, son. He may have a relapse. Or there may be complications. No, we had better see the doctor anyway, to be on the safe side.

Gosh. Your attitude toward Mr. O'Malley sure has changed, hasn't it, Pop?

Copyright 1943 Field Publications

CROCKETT JOHNSON

Mr. O'Malley, Pop thinks even if you are cured of your loss of memory I ought to tell the doctor all about it . Why don't you come along yourself .. Here's his card—

My time's awfully valuable, m'boy.

Of course, it WAS an interesting case .. I dare say, unique in the annals of medicine ... Doubtless the doctor is eager to learn the details of the method I employed to effect so miraculous a cure ...

CROCKETT JOHNSON

I suppose I shall be expected to read a paper before the medical association ... I can see myself holding the assembled medicos spellbound with my knowledge ... advancing the science of healing countless years ...

The name of O'Malley revered by a grateful humanity with the great names of medicine— Robinson, Muni, Hersholt, Barrymore! Yes, m'boy, I'll see you there tomorrow.

But, say! I don't see why a CHILD PSYCHOLOGIST is so interested in my case.

Copyright 1943 Field Publications

Mr. O'Malley, my Fairy Godfather, probably got here away ahead of us, Pop... He can fly quite fast...

A A Smith Ph D
Child Psychologist

PRIVATE
CONSULTATION
BY
APPOINTMENT

9-12

The doctor will see you in just a moment.

Gosh, Mr. O'Malley is not here yet...

CROCKETT JOHNSON

He must have been delayed, son... But you can tell the doctor all about his case.

Will you come in now, please.

But the doc would probably be a lot more interested if he saw Mr. O'Malley in person, Mom.

No doubt about THAT, Barnaby.

Copyright 1942 Field Publications

126

127

This blackboard technique may aid us in finding what causes Barnaby to believe he has this Fairy Godfather.

Hey, Doc. I put those dopey blocks together . . .

Fine, Barnaby. Now draw something on the blackboard . . . anything you like . . . I'll be in there right away.

Okay, Doc.

I'm drawing Pop.

Hello, Barnaby.

POP

Sorry I'm late . . . Got into the wrong window and I had to spend some time apologizing to a lady in a— Where's the Doc?

Mr. O'Malley!

POP

Copyright 1943 Field Publications

CROCHETT JOHNSON

The Doc's inside with Pop and Mom. He's had me playing with blocks and counting pennies and showing him which is my right ear and which is my left foot and telling him a red hunk of paper is red and a green—

Sounds like an eccentric

POP

So many of these doctors ARE . . . I know an eminent surgeon . He's an amateur magician . . . Taught him my card trick . Keeps wanting me to tell him how to saw a lady in half.

Hmmm— Blocks.

The Doc had me pile them up like that.

He'll prefer this arrangement...I did something like it years ago in our A & P store I patronized...When the clerks opened up in the morning they were so delighted with the idea that from that day on...

CROCKETT JOHNSON

...From that day on—

What have you there? Marbles?

130

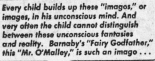

135

This "Fairy Godfather" your son believes he sees and speaks to is without doubt the idealized parent every child creates in his unconscious mind ... In the case of boys it is usually patterned after the father ... In some way you have failed to fulfill this ideal and Barnaby has allowed the fantasy to intrude upon his consciousness. It's something you can easily remedy.

Can I grow wings ... ?

CROCKETT JOHNSON Copyright 1943 Hold Publications

Make yourself more glamorous in the child's eyes ... Spend more time with him ... You'll soon take his mind off this imaginary O'Malley.

But you DON'T pay enough attention to the child ... I've always said ...

A A SMITH, Ph D
CHILD PSYCHOLOGIST

Too bad the Doc never did get to meet Mr. O'Malley.

As part of the campaign to glamorize myself and take Barnaby's mind off that non-existent Fairy Godfather, I bought him that airplane he's wanted.

Here he comes.

Hello, son. Still want that real model pursuit plane?

Gosh, Pop! Sure!

I put it under his bed. I'll go up and wave a magic wand and tell him I made it appear . . . Of course I'll explain later that I put it there.

CROCKETT JOHNSON

Hello Mr. O'Malley! Are you leaving?

I was merely examining it and it flew out there! But I'll get it back . . .

Get what back?

I don't get it! I put the toy plane under Barnaby's bed to surprise him. When I looked half an hour later it was gone! Barnaby says he doesn't know anything about it.

I've corrected a few of the more glaring aerodynamic faults I discovered as I flight-tested it just now.... Stand back, m'boy. It's wound up again...

Mr O'Malley! An airplane!

Copyright 1942 Field Publications

CROCKETT JOHNSON

A toy airplane couldn't just fly out of the house by itself, could it?

But, Pop. Mr O'Malley was testing the airplane and it flew through the window He says it was the designer's fault ..The ailerons—

Barnaby. Go to your room!

Instead of taking Barnaby's mind off his imaginary Fairy Godfather, you've made things worse ...I think you had better drop the subject of that toy plane and try to interest him in something else ...

Okay! I'll think of something ...

Remember what the psychologist said was the reason for Barnaby's abnormal imagination and what he told you—

John! Did you say the doctor could—

Fly a kite? The doctor? No. Barnaby and me. I'll buy one tomorrow and we'll fly it ...But you've got an idea there ...

CROCKETT JOHNSON

Copyright 1942 Field Publications

We couldn't get the kite up in the air. I'll add about this much to the tail and then I think it will be all right.

After all you told Barnaby about your kite-flying ability.

If Barnaby sees his father experience failures it won't help him forget about his wonderful "Fairy Godfather" ...

He's not thinking about imaginary "Mr. O'Malleys" ...

He's engrossed in our little problem. And he's perfectly convinced that if I can't fly this kite, NOBODY can ...

What's more, it's TRUE!

CROCKETT JOHNSON

Look, Pop. Mr. O'Malley got the kite up for you.

Copyright 1962 Field Publications

143

While I'm down in the cellar setting up those electric trains, I'll casually tell Barnaby I'm now warden of this whole air raid sector. He'll be so impressed with his father's importance that he won't think of his "Fairy Godfather."

10-8

...and in a blackout, I've got to see that the lights in the whole neighborhood go out promptly.

Gosh, it's a big job, isn't it? ... The other end goes in there ...

Yes, son. A very big job.

But you'll be able to do it all right, Pop ...

CROCKETT JOHNSON

... I'll get Mr. O'Malley, my Fairy Godfather, to help you ... Can I play with the trains now?

The fuse must have blown just as the raid siren sounded ... I'll fix it when the test is over ... We have to get to our air raid posts ... I'll get Barnaby.

You'd better hurry to headquarters ... You're the Sector Warden ...

Barnaby ... Put a coat on and sit on the porch until your mother and I return ... Take this flashlight but don't use it near a window or outdoors.

Okay, Pop.

Copyright 1942 Field Publications

Let's hurry, dear ... This is the first blackout since I've been Sector Warden and I want it to be a 100 percent success.

Well, OUR house is surely blacked out.

But Pop said to sit here, Mr. O'Malley.

I think we could put this time to something a bit more constructive, m'boy.

Pop said he'd put a new fuse in after the blackout is over, Mr. O'Malley...

He'll be tired after performing his air warden duties...

But I don't know where they are... Maybe we haven't got an extra fuse.

Such a household... Well, it's lucky you have a resourceful Fairy Godfather...

CROCKETT JOHNSON

Don't show the flashlight out the window, Mr. O'Malley... Pop wants the first blackout since he got to be Sector Warden to be 100 percent

Copyright 1943 Field Publications

Shake the bank harder, Barnaby. As soon as a nickel falls out I'll show you an amazing bit of electrical engineering.

Zone Headquarters? Sector 13 reporting ... We're completely blacked out ... Not a crack of light showing anywhere five minutes after the first siren sounded.

Congratulations, Commander.

Congratulations to every warden on the job ... Smythe, did you hear how our house got blacked out tonight? The main fuse blew out just as the alarm began sounding ...

All we could do was put Barnaby on the porch instead of in the blackout room and rush to our posts. We knew this was a test and everything would be okay.

Let's step outside and admire our blackout.

Hold the light steady, Barnaby, until your Fairy Godfather gets this nickel in the fuse box. We'll surprise your dad.

But Mr. O'Malley ..

CROCKETT JOHNSON

Just a minute, Barnaby. There's no sense leaving this nickel in the fuse box if all the bulbs are blown out ... And there's an intriguing new machine at the Little Men's Club ... A game of skill

I'll put back the burnt-out fuse so your father will have it to show the merchant how shoddy his products are ...

There! All shipshape!

What are we going to do? With all the bulbs burned out ...

Candlelight has its charms, m'boy ... Peace and tranquillity will descend upon this home with the warm and mellow glow of clustered tapers ...

I heard Mom and Pop come in ...

CROCKETT JOHNSON

Copyright 1942 Field Publications

Don't get grease from that awful candle over things!

Where's that kid? ...BARNABY!

Well, m'boy, your Fairy Godfather must be going.

154

The blackout was absolutely perfect—except for OUR house! And I'm the Sector Warden! I'll never live it down!

Oh, John. Things like this can happen to everybody.

I examined the blown-out fuse. I don't see how the lights came on again for five minutes... unless .. as the metal cooled it contracted ... and the current arced and blew the bulbs .. No ..

Pop, Mr. O'Malley, my Fairy Godfather, put a nickel in the fuse.

Run along to bed, Barnaby. There wasn't anything in the socket. Only the burnt fuse ... Now if an arc—

He took the nickel with him to try his skill on a machine at his club...

Don't make up stories like that, Barnaby ...

I wonder if things like this CAN happen to everybody!

CROCKETT JOHNSON

Copyright 1942 Field Publications

155

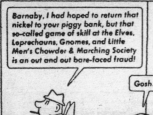

Barnaby, I had hoped to return that nickel to your piggy bank, but that so-called game of skill at the Elves, Leprechauns, Gnomes, and Little Men's Chowder & Marching Society is an out and out bare-faced fraud!

Gosh.

On my first two balls I amassed the promising total of 9,700,000,000 points. I needed 20,300,000,000, merely, on my remaining three shots to win a cool three nickels... I took careful aim... I released the plunger... And pink lights flashed "TILT"!

I complained to the club steward to no avail... I should have fought against the installation of that mechanical robber when the Leprechaun faction proposed it... Anything a Leprechaun has anything to do with means trouble!

What is a Leprechaun, Mr. O'Malley?

A Leprechaun, m'boy, is a — But, come! Let's go down to the south side of the woods and I'll point one out to you Of course, you won't become involved in any trouble when your Fairy Godfather is with you.

The average person's ignorance and misinformation about Leprechauns, Barnaby, is shocking . . . Of course, very little dependable data of any sort exists and no scientific field work has been done among them.

In some quarters they are believed to be the shoemakers and tradesmen of the Fairy World . . . Small business men—they're only a span high . . . But actually they're a shiftless lot.

Then again, they are alleged to possess the secret of fabulous wealth and to divulge it to the person who catches them . . . The nonsense people will believe! . . . I caught a Leprechaun years ago.

After I let him go, exasperated and not a farthing the richer, I discovered that my watch —

But there's one of them now! On that toadstool!

Copyright 1942 Field Publications

CROCKETT JOHNSON

158

I can hear that Leprechaun, McSnoyd, down at the Little Men's Society telling the members I waved my wand and accidently made myself invisible . . . And how he'll exaggerate the thing!

How could he exaggerate it, Mr. O'Malley?

10-20

Launcelot McSnoyd could exaggerate anything. Even the present war . . . And the fellows at the club are such a great bunch of kidders . . . I won't dare show my face there for a—

You can't, anyway.

I suppose you told your father I had something to do with the lights going on during that blackout . . . So I'd better stay hidden in the cellar . . .

Copyright 1943 Field Publications

But I'm invisible! Why I can roam the entire house now, can't I, m'boy . . . Suppose we take a look in the icebox . . .

CROCKETT JOHNSON

We'd better start figuring how we can make you visible again, Mr. O'Malley.

Very tasty avocado aspic.. Yes, m'boy, I've been giving the problem some thought.

10-27

I'll have to get hold of another copy of the Fairy Godfathers' Handy Pocket Guide .. Perhaps your father will be good enough to pick one up downtown ...

Aren't they hard to get?

I ran across my copy at the remainder counter in one of the chain drug stores ...Liggett's, I think it was ...Only copy they had ... Hmm—apple pie .. There's no great rush about that book.

I'll tiptoe past your father in the library and borrow one of his cigars ... Don't worry about my unfortunate plight, m'boy. I'll bear up under it ...

CROCKETT JOHNSON

Copyright 1943 Field Publications

Did you turn off the concert for this boxing match, John?

And a left And a right And another left And another right And—

I didn't touch the radio.

Where's that mystery story? I put it down here when you called me ... Now it's gone! I'd just reached the climax!

Don't look at me!

And you left this cigar burning on the cabinet!

Me? I'm smoking a pipe!

CROCKETT JOHNSON

I think I'll run down to Paddy's Tavern, Barnaby ... It occurred to me that I can approach the free lunch without being scowled at, now that I'm invisible ... And things are a bit dull around here.

Okay, Mr. O'Malley.

I wish Mr. O'Malley, my Fairy Godfather would get visible again ... Gosh! It's time he got back ... I've got to let him in ... He'll throw a pebble at my window ... I'll open it and he'll climb up the trellis—

What's that!

A stone!

Some kid, dolled up in a big overcoat, wearing a ridiculous falseface ... Some pink things on his back ... No bigger than Barnaby and out at this hour!

He was visible?

Copyright 1942 Field Publications

... Throwing rocks through windows and pulling down trellises ... That's carrying Hallowe'en a little too far! ... He got away fast ... He fairly flew!

Pop! You could see him? ...

CROCKETT JOHNSON

168

Of course I didn't throw that rock through the glass, Barnaby. It was McSnoyd and his crude sense of humour... Embarrassing me.

That invisible Leprechaun! He was with you?

Just as I found myself losing my invisibility from the chemical reaction of a combination of all the ingredients on Paddy's free lunch counter, I became aware of that McSnoyd's poisonous presence, and all evening he—

Let's go and tell Pop you didn't do it.

M'boy. When your Fairy Godfather tosses a pebble at a window, there aren't any accidents. I carefully calculate the resiliency of the pane ...Select a stone exactly right in weight ...Gently propel it...

CROCKETT JOHNSON

...accurately—

CRASH

Gosh! Run, Mr. O'Malley!

And another thing that Leprechaun did forced me to leave Paddy's Bar and Grill ... I was standing near the free lunch, inconspicuously—because Paddy's attitude has not been all you might expect of a good host toward a guest—and McSnoyd, still invisible, sidled up to me. ... Waiting for a lull in the conversation, the little bum did a quick but loud tap dance! ... Two chaps turned, stared at me, set down their glasses and ran out of the place! ... Paddy was quite insulting, "O'Malley! Two more of my best customers! They seen you! Get out of my establishment and stay out!"

I retorted that I was about to transfer my patronage to Duffy's Tavern in any case, and I left with dignity ... But the invisible McSnoyd kept circling me, tap-tappity-tap-tapping, as I strode out ...

How did you finally get rid of him, Mr. O'Malley?

CROCKETT JOHNSON

He's still with you!

Tap, tappity, tap, tap—TAP! TAP!

Mother: I'll bet we can get Barnaby interested in this children's scrap metal drive ... It will be a real activity and he won't be able to drag that imaginary "Fairy Godfather" into it ... What do you say?

Father: Well, let's try it.

11-6

Father: Barnaby, the children in the county are having a contest to see who can collect the most old metal. You're too little to win it but you could get some. It all helps ... A Georgie Masters, Jr., eleven years, brought in 1400 pounds of metal ... Just imagine!

Barnaby: He must be pretty strong for his age.

Father: He didn't carry it all at once, Barnaby ... And they send a truck out for any heavy pieces the children find. It all counts on their score ... Do you think you knew where there may be any old metal?

Barnaby: I think so, Pop. Are gold and silver any good?

CROCKETT JOHNSON

Father: No. So don't bother looking for any twenty dollar gold pieces.

Barnaby: Gosh. I better go tell Mr. O'Malley, my Fairy Godfather, so he won't waste the whole day!

Copyright 1942 Field Publications

173

Hey, Mr. O'Malley! Pop says if we do find that Leprechaun's treasure, it's no good—

Your father must have been joking.

No. The Government's got a whole lot of gold ... It needs scrap iron.

Let's find McSnoyd's treasure anyway, m'boy ... If what you say is true, I'll solicit the services of an unemployed alchemist friend who lives near by ...

Copyright 1943 Field Publications

He and I accidently discovered a method —which he was generous enough to call "The O'Malley Process"—of successfully transforming gold into baser metals ...

But here we are ... There's the Leprechaun's toadstool!

CROCKETT JOHNSON

174

When that shiftless McSnoyd returns and finds his treasure gone it will serve him right . . . Teach him to pay a bit more attention to his Leprechaun business and not go running about annoying people.

I don't see any treasure, Mr. O'Malley. Maybe he hasn't any after all.

Abide by your Fairy Godfather's sound judgment in these matters. Besides I have a hunch it's here.

Mr. O'Malley! Look!

Found the treasure already! Good work! Don't attempt to lift it. All that gold—

Copyright 1943 Field Publications

Part of an egg beater! For the scrap iron drive.

CROCKETT JOHNSON

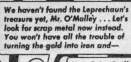

We haven't found the Leprechaun's treasure yet, Mr. O'Malley . . . Let's look for scrap metal now instead. You won't have all the trouble of turning the gold into iron and—

Your Fairy Godfather doesn't admit defeat so easily, Barnaby.

I shall match cunning with cunning . . . When McSnoyd arrives I'll trick him into betting he can answer questions truthfully. If he does, we'll know where the treasure is . . . If he doesn't—well, I can use a couple of extra smokes . . .

You'll bet him a couple of cigars?

Copyright 1943 Field Publications

When he gets here, I'll say, "McSnoyd, I'll wager you two clear Havana cigars—

Okay, O'Malley. I'll take you up.

The invisible Leprechaun! He's here already, Mr. O'Malley!

. . . Two clear Havana cigars—None of them terrible stogies you usually smoke, Pal.

Let me sniff them cheroots, O'Malley.

Listen, you invisible old Leprechaun! . . . They're my father's best cigars . . .

Hmmm. Not bad. Okay. It's a bet . . . The truth. . . . Nothing excepting the truth.

This is easy, Barnaby . . . Now look, McSnoyd, is it true you're guarding jewels and silver and gold and—

Well, it's like this. All us Leprechauns used to have to guard treasures, like in the kids' books . . . Took all our time . . . We didn't have no fun or no recreation . . .

So we made this here moiger. We got rid of all the silver and the poils and cut-glass junk and now we take toins guarding one big pile of solid 24-karat gold . . . You never seen such a heap. Tons and tons and tons and tons—

Remember, McSnoyd Nothing but the truth.

Sure. Tons and tons and tons— Come on. I'll SHOW it to you.

There's some catch to this Mr. O'Malley.

We ought to be picking up scrap iron, Mr. O'Malley, instead of following that invisible Leprechaun just because he says he's got tons and tons of gold.

Tons and tons and TONS . . .

I haven't noticed any scrap iron lying about, m'boy. I imagine people have found it and turned it all in by now.

Pop says that's the trouble . . . There's plenty, but nobody notices it . . .

. . . tons and tons and . . .

CROCKETT JOHNSON

Your Fairy Godfather's powers of observation are terrific, m'boy, and if I haven't noticed any scrap iron—

Say, McSnoyd. How much farther is that treasure? This isn't that old end-of-the-rainbow gag, I hope.

Feet hoit, O'Malley?

Copyright 1942 Field Publications

Let's rest a moment beside this old abandoned steamroller . . . Now as I was saying, Barnaby, if I don't notice any scrap iron—

Mr. O'Malley! A genuine iron steamroller!

Yes ... A steamroller ... "Trilby. Ten Tons. Patented 1908" ... An old model and the boiler's blown out ... Bit rusty, too ... But if the scrap committee isn't too fussy—

Is ten tons more than 1400 pounds, Mr. O'Malley?

11·13

Let me see ... Carry the two ... I'm making a lightning mathematical calculation ... Both heavy sums, but ten tons is somewhat weightier ...

Okay. So you don't want to see them tons and tons of gold, O'Malley?

Copyright 1943 Field Publications

Of course I do, McSnoyd ... Barnaby, you tell the salvage committee about the steamroller and I'll investigate this invisible Leprechaun's treasure.

Gosh. The boy in first place in the kid's scrap contest only has found 1400 pounds of metal.

I mean the boy who WAS in first place.

Shake a leg, O'Malley ...

CROCKETT JOHNSON

Hey, Pop! I found some scrap iron . . .

11-14   Copyright 1942 Field Publications

I knew we could get Barnaby interested in the children's scrap contest even if he is too young to really compete.

I found a piece of tire chain and part of an egg beater and a steamroller named Trilby.

Fine, Barnaby. Every few ounces help—

CROCKETT JOHNSON

. . . and a WHAT?

A steamroller.

Barnaby was right about that ten-ton steamroller! . . . It's lying out there in the woods, overgrown with weeds, near that winding section of road they cut off when they built the new highway—

Sure . . . Gosh, didn't you believe me, Pop?

Of course I believed you, Barnaby. But a steamroller! I just wanted to see it myself before we phoned the salvage committee about it. But I believed you.

Tell them I may have a lot more if Mr. O'Malley, my Fairy Godfather, finds the tons and tons of gold a Leprechaun we met told him about . . . Mr. O'Malley knows how to change gold into iron . . .

CROCKETT JOHNSON

Don't you believe me again, Pop?

Here's a story about how they're going to salvage that ten-ton steamroller you found, Barnaby. And the way the leaders stand in the scrap iron contest.

"Barnaby Baxter, 20,000 ½ pounds, first— Georgie Masters, Jr., 1427 pounds, second —Howard Clark, 980 — Say, son, you don't seem to be very happy about all this . . .

Mr. O'Malley, my Fairy Godfather, hasn't come back yet. I'm worried.

Listen to this! The winner of the contest will make a little speech on the RADIO, with — guess who with!

Fred Allen?

Copyright 1942 Field Publications

The MAYOR!

Oh.

CROCKETT JOHNSON

Even winning the children's scrap iron contest and getting to do a broadcast with the Mayor isn't taking Barnaby's mind off that imaginary "Mr. O'Malley."

11-18

I can't understand it. Except for this one silly obsession, he's a very rational youngster . . . Even bright.

What possible explanation is there for his persistent belief that a "Fairy Godfather" with wings comes to visit him?

CROCKETT JOHNSON

Mr. O'Malley!

Hello, Barnaby.

Copyright 1942 Field Publications

I won the kid's scrap collecting contest, Mr. O'Malley, and I'm going to be on the radio . . . The Mayor and I are going to be—

Radio?

I might come along myself, Barnaby, and have a try at a few of those $64 questions—

But it's not a quiz program

Then tell Charlie McCarthy he need look no farther for his next week's guest star . . . I'll be glad to—

It's just me and the Mayor . . . We're going to make speeches.

CROCKETT JOHNSON

Copyright 1942 Field Publications

Speeches? Right up your Fairy Godfather's alley! I'll deliver something appropriate . . . Perhaps a fragment from my most recent filibuster at the Elves, Leprechauns, Gnomes, & Little Men's Chowder & Marching Society.

Come along, Barnaby. Even a champion scrap collector isn't important enough to keep a radio program waiting . . .

Mom. Mr. O'Malley, my Fairy Godfather, will be at the broadcast . . .

11-21

Barnaby! You're not going to babble about that little man with the pink wings in front of the Mayor and all those people at the radio station!

But if he's there, I'll have to introduce him to everybody, won't I?

IF he's there . . . But until he does get there — not another word about him!

But Mr. O'Malley is going to — Oh, okay, Pop, okay!

CROCKETT JOHNSON

That's it. Goodbye, Son. I'll listen to every word of your broadcast. Everything's going to be fine . . .

Well, I hope so.

So this is the winner of the scrap collecting contest . . . Congratulations . . . Just be seated . . . The Mayor will be here any minute and we'll go up to the broadcasting room.

11-23

Mr. O'Malley, my Fairy Godfather, should be here any minute, too—

Barnaby!

Okay—I forgot . . . I can't say anything about him until he actually arrives.

Mom. Do Mayors always wear firemen's hats or—Listen!

Sorry if I'm a bit tardy . . . Several very momentous matters detained me . . .

. . . Demanded my personal attention . . . Had to make several decisions of very paramount importance . . .

Mom! He's here! Mr. O'Malley!

CROCKETT JOHNSON

Barnaby! That's not your imaginary Fairy Godfather! It's the MAYOR!

... Auspicious occasion ...

It IS Mr. O'Malley!

11-24   Copyright 1942 Field Publications

I've composed a very stirring speech ... Should hold the radio audience spellbound ...

Barnaby!

Hey, Mr. O'Malley!

CROCKETT JOHNSON

Barnaby, this is His Honor, the Mayor.

Delighted, m'boy.

We'll go right to the broadcasting studio.

Gosh, Mr. Hizzonner, you talk exactly like my—

Hey! What's the big rush, Mom?

These are times when nobody can sit idly twiddling his thumbs . . .

11-25

. . . and the little boy who I am about to introduce—the winner of the children's scrap contest—sets us all an example!

Maybe Mr. O'Malley, my Fairy Godfather, couldn't find the studio . . . I'll just look down the hall once and see if—

Pssssst! Barnaby!

Mr. O'Malley!

STUDIO F

ON THE AIR

CROCKETT JOHNSON

Give ear to the strains of this Duke Ellington opus, m'boy . . . Sizzling but solid—as we cognizant felidae say—

RECORDING

Copyright 1942 Field Publications

189

And now it is our privilege to hear from the surprisingly young winner of the children's scrap iron contest,

BARNABY BAXTER!

Where IS the child?

What could have—

He was right here—

Here he is!

He was out of the studio!

Hello, everybody. We should all collect scrap iron and we should all buy War Stamps and Bonds. I also wish you a very happy Thanksgiving . . .

My Fairy Godfather, Mr. O'Malley, was going to make a speech, too, but he says the Mayor took all the words right out of his mouth so he will play a record instead—Hey!

Ouch, Mom! My arm—

CROCKETT JOHNSON

190

You heard Barnaby's broadcast?

Yes. I heard it.

I talked right out of the radio like that lady singer! Gosh!

♪ — There are — ♪ Fairies at the bottom of ♪ my gar-den...

Why did you say those nonsensical things about your "Fairy Godfather"?

He was there, Pop. And Mom wouldn't stay to meet him!

♪ — Oh they DOOO? ♪ Yes they DOO-OOO ♪

This "Mr. O'Malley" with his pink wings was at the radio station? ... Who saw him—besides you.

Nobody, I guess ... But he was there—

♪ — And the queen — ♪ ♪ — of the fairies ♪

CROCKETT JOHNSON

♪ The queen of the fairies ♪ — is MEEE — EEEEEEEK! CUSHLAMOCHREE!

Mr. O'Malley! He's still there!

... because of Madam deCibel's sudden indisposition. For the remainder of this quarter hour we bring you a recorded series of seventeenth-century compositions for the harpsichord ... the first, by Scarlatti, is entitled —

Barnaby. What would your "Fairy Godfather" be doing at a radio station?

11-28

BOOGIE-WOOGIE MAMA'S GOT THE BLOOOS—

Click!

Hey, Joe! Who's at the turntable?

Ahem. During this slight delay, a very important message from the sponsor—

BOOGIE-WOOGIE MAMA—

The studio lights! They're out! Hey! What's going on in that control room!

BANG! BANG! RAT A TAT TAT! The Red Onion Gang! They're following us in the next gondola through this Tunnel of Love, Chief ... BANG! BANG! RAT A TAT TAT—

BOOGIE-WOOGIE MAMA! SQUAWK!

... brings you his forceful analysis of the news ... Good evening. Is there a world situation? This question cannot be answered by a simple yes or no. On one hand—

Kiddies, tell Mama to hop out now and buy fifty boxes of Stuffo! Send the box tops and two dollars from your piggy bank, to cover cost of mailing, for a lovely photo of your Uncle Ben for the parlor mantel ... Ladies and gentlemen. Due to circumstances

SCREEEEEECH!

CUSHLAMOCHREE!

This is the everyday story of a beautiful and talented girl lumberjack and her search for happiness ... As Joan learns that her mother's Phi Bata Kappa key has been discovered in the hand of the murdered East Indian prince, she redoubles her efforts to get out of the beartrap fate flung in her path—

CUSHLAMOCHREE!

BOOGIE-WOOGIE BOOGIE—

SQUAWK!

BOOGIE-WOOGIE MAMA!

beyond our control we are going off the air—

Please stand by ...

CROCKETT JOHNSON Copyright 1942 Field Publications

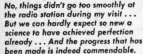

No, things didn't go too smoothly at the radio station during my visit . . . But we can hardly expect so new a science to have achieved perfection already . . . And the progress that has been made is indeed commendable.

People take the miracle of radio for granted nowadays. They forget how, a few short years ago when the idea of transmitting sound without wires was attempted, they laughed at Amos 'n' Andy . . . It just goes to show, m'boy.

What goes to show what, Mr. O'Malley?

Yes, doesn't it? . . . Speaking of new things, I see a new family has moved into that house down the road . . .

Copyright 1942 Field Publications

Maybe we ought to call on them.

Your Fairy Godfather was toying with the same idea, Barnaby.

CROCKETT JOHNSON

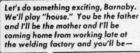

You're sure you don't want me to change a pumpkin into a slick convertible with five white-wall tires for the little girl? I can't do that though, can I? You haven't got a pumpkin... Perhaps if I—

12-8

No. Just come by and let her see you, Mr. O'Malley. She won't believe I've got a Fairy Godfather and —

A skeptical child, isn't she, m'boy?

CROCKETT JOHNSON

But like Pop says, Seeing is Believing, huh, Mr. O'Malley?

Or vice versa...

Believing is Seeing is the way I put it... Same idea of course.... Now, Barnaby, you engage the little girl in some childish pursuit and I'll stroll by...

There's Jane, now.

...and your little girl will be a help in curbing Barnaby's wild imagination...

Jane's always been a perfect little realist... Why, do you know, when she first heard of Santa Claus, she said—

Hey, Mama. Barnaby's Fairy Godfather can't really exist, can he?

No, dear... He's purely imaginary.

That's what I told him and he got very angry and he said he wouldn't finish doing his old card trick but it wasn't coming out right anyway and then→

Barnaby was doing card tricks, Jane?

Copyright 1942 Field Publications

No... Mr. O'Malley. Barnaby's imaginary Fairy Godfather.

CROCKETT JOHNSON

202

Jane, don't be exasperating. Barnaby's Fairy Godfather is imaginary. You know that. How could you have seen him?

You just imagined you saw him, didn't you?

But . . .

12-11

Little men with wings can't exist. And you can't see imaginary things. So you didn't really see him . . . Now run out and play with Barnaby . . .

And don't let him talk you into seeing things.

But . . .

CROCKETT JOHNSON

Gosh, Jane, it's like my Fairy Godfather says . . . People will think you're nuts if you go around imagining you don't see things when—how's that, Mr. O'Malley?

When confronted by empirical evidence . . . And I might add—

But . . .

WHAAAH!

Cushlamochree!

Gosh!

Barnaby got Jane so overwrought with his stories about his "Fairy Godfather" that she imagined she actually saw him twice . . . She became hysterical . . . Her mother is terribly upset by it all.

Maybe I ought to drop in there and sort of apologize and explain about Barnaby's silly fixation—if I can . . .

I think it will be a nice gesture . . .

Cases like that often require skilled analysis to find what is causing the trouble . . . And parents can't seem to keep up with all the latest tenets of child psychology . . . I think I ought to run over there myself, Barnaby.

CROCKETT JOHNSON

It's barely possible even that I have been the cause of the little girl's tantrum . . . I may have frustrated her by not completing my amazing card trick . . . Which is her window?

Jane! What's the matter!

He was here! Mr. O'Malley! Barnaby's imaginary Fairy Godfather! Right here!

Nobody was here, Jane . . . Why did you open the window?

Mr. O'Malley opened it! He came in and went out that way!

He said he'd do a card trick and he told me, "Take a card . . ."

You were dreaming, Jane . . . Mama will sit here while you go back to sleep—

Look, Mama! It wasn't a dream! Here's the card!

CROCKETT JOHNSON

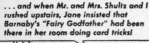

... and when Mr. and Mrs. Shultz and I rushed upstairs, Jane insisted that Barnaby's "Fairy Godfather" had been there in her room doing card tricks!

Nobody could convince her it was only a dream. And the worst of it was she had a card in her hand she said Mr. O'Malley gave her.

Where did she get that?

Picked it up somewhere during the day and didn't remember it, I guess. Just an ordinary dirty old playing card ... But anyway, now she's sure "Mr. O'Malley" is real ... She's just as convinced as our Barnaby is.

CROCKETT JOHNSON

Copyright 1942 Field Publications

Poor Mr. and Mrs. Shultz ...

A LITTLE BIT OF HISTORY...

by Ron Goulart

The 1940s was not an overly cheerful period, with such less than laughable events as the Second World War and the dawn of the Nuclear Age. Not surprisingly most of the memorable comic strips that came along in that decade were on the serious side—new detective strips like *Rip Kirby* and *Kerry Drake*, new adventure strips like *Johnny Hazard* and *Steve Canyon*. Somehow, though, two of the best humor strips of the century managed to get born in the 1940s as well. They were Walt Kelly's *Pogo* and *Barnaby*.

In the spring of 1942, just a few months after the United States entered World War II, *Barnaby* began appearing in the liberal New York tabloid *PM*. One of the best-drawn and best-written strips of the decade, it was cooked up by a man who had little interest in or liking for comics. Crockett Johnson, who'd begun life some 36 years earlier as David Johnson Leisk, was the creator of the strip. He later explained that his prime motivation was a desire to find something that would guarantee him a steady income. Before he sold *Barnaby*, a task that took two years, he'd earned a less-than-handsome living doing department-store advertising art and then cartoons for magazines like *Collier's*.

In a little more than a year after its modest debut, *Barnaby* was in syndication with a growing list of major newspapers, had been reprinted in a handsome hardcover book, and was being raved about by such mainstream periodicals as *Time, Newsweek,* and *Life*, which called it "a breath of cool, sweet air."

*From *Funnies in the 40's—Part 2*, by Ron Goulart, which first appeared in Summer 1985 Newsstand Quarterly *Comics Collector*. ©1985 Krause Publications. Used by permission.

Furthermore, a raft of influential intellectuals had fallen under the strip's spell and made the fact public. Dorothy Parker called it "the most important addition to American arts and letters in Lord knows how many years." Robert Nathan, Rockwell Kent, Louis Untermeyer, Norman Corwin, and William Rose Benet were all equally enthusiastic. W.C. Fields was quoted as saying, "Barnaby is a whiz."

The strip that generated all this excited response was unlike anything that had ever popped up on comic pages. Johnson's drawing style, inspired by the simple and effective work of men like Gluyas Williams, accomplished a great deal with just outline and flat blacks. There was no noodling, feathering, or shading to be seen, and Johnson relied almost entirely on medium and long shots. Everything—people, animals, trees, buildings, automobiles—was drawn flat and dimensionless. He achieved a feeling of perspective the same way a paper cutout diorama does.

Although some historians have characterized Johnson's drawing as static and lacking in action, it was not so. He often used chases, slapstick struggles, and other devices assimilated from the movie comedies he was fond of. He was also very good at suggesting character and attitude, conveying anguish, frustration, self-importance, etc. with a few deft lines. A typographer on the side, Johnson set his dialogue in a distinctive, lower-case, sans-serif type. This may've saved a little time, but his main reason was a desire to fit more copy into his balloons. He often used a hundred or more words in a daily. (The average in most of today's humor strips is in the neighborhood of 25.)

The co-stars of the strip were Barnaby (a bright and articulate preschooler), and Mr. O'Malley (his windy and not completely effectual Fairy Godfather). O'Malley, a child-size, pudgy fellow in an overcoat that allowed his pink wings to flap freely, used a Havana cigar as a magic wand and never encountered a problem, large or small, he wasn't ready to tackle—or at least discuss, sometimes at great length, tackling. O'Malley, saving his magical powers for a last resort, was a great one for drawing up complicated plans and intricate charts. He was also fond of polls and telephone surveys. In other words, he was a pixie who believed in blending ancient sorceries with the latest public relations techniques.

Mr. O'Malley showed up on the strip's second day, after Barnaby, inspired by a fairy tale his mother read him, wished for a fairy godmother. Instead he got Jackeen J. O'Malley, who came flying in the open bedroom window, made a less-than-perfect landing, and bent his stogie. "Cushlamochree! Broke my magic wand!...Lucky Boy! Your wish is granted! I'm your Fairy Godfather."

The boy's initial comment was a simple, awed, "Gosh!"

O'Malley went on to assure him, "Yes, m'boy, your troubles are over. O'Malley is on the job." Introductions over, he promised to return and flew out the window. This dramatic exit was spoiled some by the fact that he crashed in the shrubs below.

Barnaby's parents rushed up to see what was going on. He attempted to explain his marvelous visitor—"He's got pink wings! He can grant wishes!"—but his father, adopting the attitude he would hold onto for the run of the strip, told him, "Try not to dream anymore, son."

After they left him, Barnaby remembered Mr. O'Malley's cigar. He hopped out of bed and, sure enough, found ashes on his floor. From that moment he, and the reader, knew that O'Malley was real.

Forget, by the way, what you may have read elsewhere. Barnaby didn't live in a fantasy world. He lived in the real world, as perceived by a smart preschool kid. It's a remarkable place where reality and fantasy can comfortably co-exist. Despite his parents' concerns and criticisms, he was extremely practical and not a dreamer at all. And, although he was fond of his flamboyant Fairy Godfather, he could be critical of his follies, committed or proposed.

While Barnaby avoided some of the more common physical hazards of childhood—he was rarely sick, there were no kid bullies in his venue, neither parent took a hairbrush to him—he suffered most of the pyschological ones.

His folks didn't often listen to him in anything but a critical way and they nearly always assumed his perceptions and assumptions were not only hopelessly naive but dead wrong.

One of the boy's oftfelt emotions was frustration. When he knew the truth or the answer to a question, he was rarely paid attention to or believed. His most frequently seen speech balloon over the years contained the single word "But—" That occurred in encounters with his parents ("It's all right now, Barnaby. You were dreaming." "But—") and with O'Malley ("If, and sometimes I doubt it, your parents actually do exist, I cannot but conclude they're avoiding me! Coincidence can only go so far...If I'm wrong, they can contact me at the club...I'm leaving, m'boy!" "But—").

Johnson stacked the cards in Barnaby's favor. One of the quiet ironies of the strip was that all the fantastic events that caused the Baxters to worry and fret over their son's mental state were actually happening. What Johnson seemed to be saying was that to a child the world is a much more marvelous and wonderful place than adults notice it to be. That he did this without being sticky and fey is one of the triumphs of *Barnaby*.

The supporting players were a rich and varied lot. There was Barnaby's dog, Gorgon, who could, when in the mood, talk. Gorgon was inclined toward puns and never tired of remarking that he was dog tired or led a dog's life. Once, when Gorgon was recruited to portray a dog on a radio show O'Malley put together, the critics dismissed his performance as unconvincing.

The sprawling suburban neighborhood the Baxters lived in came complete with a haunted house. The resident ghost was a timid wraith named Gus. An extremely literate spook (he even wore glasses), he was continually being conned into performing tasks for O'Malley—writing his political speeches, helping stage his version of *Hamlet*, etc.

The surrounding woods (this was the '40s, and suburban areas still had woodlands surrounding them) contained a variety of pixies, ogres, elves, and other so-called mythical creatures. There was also Launcelot McSnoyd, a somewhat uncouth leprechaun. Invisible, he held a low opinion of Mr. O'Malley and delighted in heckling him. When O'Malley first introduced him to Barnaby, the lowbrow leprechaun remarked, "Still working the Fairy Godfather racket, O'Malley."

Barnaby's contemporaries had no trouble seeing O'Malley and all the other creatures. His closest friend, Janie Schultz, considered O'Malley something of a dope and a nuisance and preferred to get her excitement from *Captain Bloodbath Comics* and stories like the one "where the mad doctor saws off the top of Captain Bloodbath's head and steals a secret code he memorized."

Mr. O'Malley was a member, not always in good standing, of the Elves, Leprechauns, Gnomes and Little Men's Chowder and Marching Society. When he was not hanging around with Barnaby, concocting a new scheme or availing himself of the leftover roast lamb almost always to be found in the Baxter refrigerator, he could be found at the group's headquarters. Or at Paddy's Bar & Grill, a convivial establishment that didn't discriminate against pixies. O'Malley's attire never varied, although he did don a different hat when he went to Congress and wore a helmet when planning a military campaign. And, of course, every winter he was to be seen with earmuffs.

Johnson was a restless man and he apparently yearned to try other things, everything from children's books to serious painting. In 1952 he announced he was discontinuing the strip and as of February 2 Barnaby and Mr. O'Malley would be seen no more. That proved, as this present volume shows, not to have been exactly true.

ABOUT THE AUTHOR

Born in New York of Scottish parents, Crockett
Johnson's only formal art training was a six-months'
stint at Cooper Union, drawing from plaster casts
and studying typography. His first job was with
Macy's advertising department, from which he
resigned—just before he was fired for wearing a soft
collar instead of the regulation stiff one.

Before settling down to work on *Barnaby* in 1942,
Johnson was art director for McGraw-Hill and a
free-lance cartoonist whose most popular feature,
"The Little Man with the Eyes," appeared regularly
in *Collier's*. His children's book—*Harold and the
Purple Crayon*—is one of the great classics.